WORDS *of* HOPE *and* HEALING

Expected Loss
COPING *with*
ANTICIPATORY
GRIEF

Alan D. Wolfelt, Ph.D.

Companion
P R E S S

An imprint of the Center for Loss and Life Transition | Fort Collins, Colorado

Companion Press is an imprint of the Center for Loss and Life Transition, 3735 Broken Bow Road, Fort Collins, Colorado 80526.

25 24 23 22 21 20   6 5 4 3 2 1

ISBN: 978-1-61722-295-5

CONTENTS

WELCOME

"The art of life lies in a constant readjustment to our surroundings."
— Kakuzo Okakura

If you are living through a time of difficult change leading to an expected loss, this book is for you.

Change is hard. Loss is hard. You need and deserve compassion and support. Thank you for allowing me the privilege of having this conversation with you during this difficult period in your life. I hope it will help you better understand and express your normal, necessary grief.

EXPECTING GRIEF

"All great changes are preceded by chaos."
— Deepak Chopra

WHAT IS GRIEF?

Before we focus on anticipatory grief, perhaps we should begin by defining grief itself. So, what is grief, anyway?

Grief is everything you think and feel inside of you after a loss of any kind. We all understand that the death of someone loved causes grief, of course, but so do other kinds of significant losses and life transitions. Divorce, job loss, relocation, estrangement or separation from friends and family, health issues, and many other common life experiences often give rise to profound grief.

Typical grief feelings include (but aren't limited to) numbness, shock, denial, confusion, disorientation, anger, guilt, relief, yearning, and sadness. Grieving people typically experience several feelings at the same time, and their emotions often change from day to day or even moment to moment.

In general, the stronger your attachment to a person, situation, or thing, the stronger your grief will be when your ties to that person, situation, or thing are severed or placed in jeopardy.

Grief is a normal and necessary part of life because change and loss are normal and unavoidable parts of life. What's more, grief is a corollary to love. In fact, grief *is* love in the face of separation or change. To live and to love as a human being is to one day grieve.

WHAT IS ANTICIPATORY GRIEF?

If grief is the inner experience of loss, anticipatory grief is the inner experience of expected loss. If you love someone who is dying, for example, you will naturally begin to anticipate their eventual death. You will likely feel many of the emotions listed above as you witness their journey and the changes they are undergoing as well as consider the many "what ifs" and "what nexts"—including imagining your life after the death.

Anticipatory grief often has two components: process and projection.

The first has to do with the process of living through change. Many big life changes and losses are not instantaneous but rather play out over the course of months or even years.

For instance, if you are caring for someone with dementia, you will begin to see that person changing in both subtle and substantial ways before your very eyes. These changes are gradual, and they may even seem to reverse at times. As the person slowly changes, your relationship with them changes, too. These changes cause grief because characteristics you were attached to are fading away and being replaced by characteristics that are new, strange, or difficult. It's as if the person you have loved is leaving you even though they are physically still there.

Other common life changes that are often drawn out over time and cause anticipatory grief include separation and divorce, the maturation and eventual independence of children, health declines due to chronic illness and/or aging, and financial downturns.

The other component of anticipatory grief has to do with the natural human tendency to project ourselves forward in time. Among animals, what best distinguishes our species is our capacity to think about the future. Our minds are powerful tools. They allow us to do many complicated tasks, including visualizing and planning for what's to come. This amazing ability is what enables us to do things like attend and complete educational courses, make family plans, and save for and imagine distant goals, like retirement. However, it can also cause us to worry, catastrophize, and spend more time and energy in our imaginations than in the present.

It's normal to think about, and yes, worry about what will happen after the loss you are anticipating is "over." Depending on the loss you are expecting, this finality might mean death, divorce, relocation, bankruptcy, etc. What's more, this projection part of your anticipatory grief may include some buoyant feelings, like hope and release. Especially if you are experiencing a painful or turbulent time of change right now, you may be looking forward to some aspects of your life stabilizing or improving after the loss. This is also understandable and normal.

And finally, keep in mind that anticipatory grief often crops up during times of normal, happy life transition. If you have a child about to graduate from high school and head off to college, for example, you may experience anticipatory grief in the months leading up to the move. The same thing can happen before a wedding, the birth of a baby, or a hoped-for career change. The common denominator is that change is hard, and we almost always grieve aspects of significant change, even when the change is something we're looking forward to.

I will also note that there's another category of loss experience that may overlap with anticipatory grief. It's called ambiguous loss. Ambiguous loss is when you find yourself grieving in loss circumstances that don't have a clear endpoint or status. For example, if a loved one struggles with long-term addiction and is in and out of sobriety, you may be living with anticipatory grief—grieving the process and projecting possible death or ruin—yet there may never be a climactic resolution of any kind. If you feel your anticipatory grief circumstances are also ambiguous, I see you, and I welcome you to this conversation.

SITUATIONS THAT CAUSE ANTICIPATORY GRIEF

Common situations that cause anticipatory grief include:

- Terminal or life-threatening illness (of someone else or of oneself)
- Dementia
- Aging
- Divorce
- Pending major medical procedures (such as mastectomy or open-heart surgery)
- Upcoming major life transitions (such as graduation, weddings, job change, or pending relocation or geographical separation)

HOW IS ANTICIPATORY GRIEF DIFFERENT FROM REGULAR GRIEF?

If we think of regular grief as what we feel inside "after" a significant change is final, and we think of anticipatory grief as what we feel inside during the process of the change, we find that they're very similar but have a few differentiating features.

First, because anticipatory grief typically begins during a period of change, it can be more chaotic and unpredictable. What's changing hasn't yet settled into its final state. You may not even know what the final outcome will be. You may be imagining a number of different possible scenarios. You might not know what to wish for. Human beings generally don't like to live in this kind of uncertainty. It's uncomfortable and disorienting.

Second, you will likely experience heightened emotions as the person or thing you are attached to undergoes this change. You might feel ferociously protective or surprisingly torn or ambivalent. You may simply wish for it to be over.

Third, because of the natural tendency to imagine, in part, happy or hopeful aspects of your future after the loss, you may experience heightened guilt at times. I call this joy-guilt because your happy, hopeful feelings might then make you feel guilty, and it's a normal feature of anticipatory grief.

And fourth, those who experience anticipatory grief come to understand that the "in-between" time they are granted is both a privilege and a hardship. If someone you love is dying, for example, the opportunity to spend those final weeks or months at their side is precious time that people who suffer the sudden death of a loved one don't get. On the other hand, sudden loss often precludes the suffering of both the person who is dying and their loved ones as well as all the pain of uncertainty along the way.

MOURNING
ANTICIPATORY GRIEF

"Don't keep all your feelings sheltered—express them.
Don't ever let life shut you up."
— Dr. Steve Maraboli

WHAT IS MOURNING?

Mourning is expressing our grief outside of ourselves. Grief is internal; mourning is external. Grief is hidden; mourning is visible. I often say that mourning is "grief gone public."

Another way to think of it is that mourning is grief in motion. And it's that quality of movement that makes it so powerful.

The wonderful thing about mourning is that it's how you integrate your grief into your life and continue to live and love well even as you're grieving. And over time, especially after the loss you're expecting reaches its endpoint, mourning is how you will come to reconcile your grief and heal.

WHAT "COUNTS" AS MOURNING?

Lots of things count as mourning!

Talking to someone else about your grief is a mainstay of mourning. Crying is another.

Did you know that our bodies produce three kinds of tears? Basal tears are the natural moisture that bathes our eyes to keep them moist and eliminate bad bacteria. Reflex tears well up when we get something annoying in our eye, like an eyelash or shampoo. But emotional tears—those are the tears that rid our bodies of stress chemicals and help us cope with high emotions, sad or happy. Those emotional tears do good mourning work.

In addition to talking to compassionate listeners and crying, you can mourn by:

- writing down your thoughts and feelings in a notebook, journal, or notecard

- emailing or texting someone

- singing along with a song that expresses your feelings

- participating in a support group

- making art

- making or doing something with your hands and body, such as gardening, cooking, or playing sports

- actively engaging with your thoughts and memories by making a photo book or memory box

- seeing a counselor

There's no right way to mourn. As long as you're expressing

your grief outside of yourself and it feels helpful or cathartic to you, you're on the right track.

THE SIX NEEDS OF MOURNING

Every grieving person who commits to active mourning finds means of expression that work for them. What works for you may not work for others, and vice versa. That's OK. Your grief is unique, and your mourning will be unique too.

But it's also true that there are certain aspects of effective mourning that we all share. I call these the "needs of mourning." As long as you're finding ways to meet all six of the central mourning needs, you are helping yourself integrate your grief.

NEED 1: ACKNOWLEDGE THE REALITY OF YOUR GRIEF AND THE PENDING LOSS

For some people, it's hard just to admit that they're grieving and that a significant loss is on the horizon. Our culture isn't very open and honest about loss, so if you've been avoiding thinking about and facing your grief and loss, you're not alone.

Yet this is an essential step on the journey to coping with anticipatory grief. Day by day, bit by bit, you must acknowledge that you are grieving and that a loss is coming. You first acknowledge this reality with your head, but over time you will come to acknowledge it with your heart.

You are strong enough to see and accept the facts of your circumstances. You are courageous enough to ask questions and hear honest answers when you are unsure about any of the facts. And you are resilient enough to trust that you will indeed survive.

If you've found yourself avoiding the reality that you are confronted with, it's time to gently introduce yourself to the truth. Talk to others who are knowledgeable about the situation and ask them to be straight with you. Share your thoughts and feelings about what is happening, no matter what they are. If there are ambiguities and uncertainties, that's OK. Relinquish the illusion of control, and don't forget to express how you feel about the reality that you can't control what is happening.

Also, learn to describe yourself as grieving. After all, you *are* grieving, and thinking of yourself in this way will help you be both self-compassionate and honest about how challenging your current circumstances are.

NEED 2: EMBRACE BOTH THE PAIN AND THE JOY OF YOUR ANTICIPATORY GRIEF

As we've discussed, anticipatory grief often includes a wide range of feelings. Many of them are uncomfortable. We generally don't want to feel confused, sad, or guilty, for instance. We might revel in feeling mad, on the other hand, because anger can seem active and temporarily creates that illusion of control we talked about a minute ago. And any happy or hopeful feelings we have can feel good—but also bewildering. How can we possibly feel happiness in the middle of such a terrible situation?

No matter what your mixture of feelings includes—a mixture that no doubt changes all the time—this mourning need is about embracing and expressing those feelings. Your emotions are legitimate and necessary. That includes any feelings of happiness, joy, and hope! Find a good listener who will be compassionate and nonjudgmental as you share how you are feeling. And try expressing your emotions in the other ways I mentioned as well.

Naming and expressing feelings softens them. When they're stuck inside you, they may seem overwhelming and unbearable. But it's almost like a magic trick—the moment you start to let them out and give them room to roam, they subside a bit. They grow less powerful and all-consuming. And you will also start to see them for what they are—facets of your love for what you may be losing.

DOSING YOUR MOURNING NEEDS

Mourning is hard work. Immersing yourself in your grief and actively expressing whatever it is you are thinking and feeling is often draining and fatiguing. It's the good kind of draining—the kind that ultimately fills you back up—but draining nonetheless.

So I want you to always remember to dose your mourning. In other words, do it a little bit at a time. Actively and intentionally express your grief for a few minutes or an hour, then give yourself a break. Go do something fun, relaxing, restful, or distracting instead.

I sometimes call this the evade-encounter dance. It works to run away from, ignore, or postpone—in other words, evade—your grief for much of the day if you also set aside time to focus on your grief and express it. You evade it, but you also encounter it in small doses, one day at a time. It's a balance that helps you cope in healthy ways but also allows you to continue to live your life as you do so.

NEED 3: EXPLORE MEMORIES ASSOCIATED WITH THE LOVE OR ATTACHMENT YOU'RE LOSING

When you're anticipating a major loss, you're naturally living in three timeframes. You're worried about the future, you're struggling in the present, and you're also likely thinking about the past, perhaps of times when things were more stable and life felt better.

This mourning need reminds you that it's normal and necessary to include those reflections of the past in your grief and mourning. In my forty years as a grief counselor and educator, I've learned that it's essential to listen to the music of the past to sing in the present and dance into the future. Another way of saying this is that in grief it's necessary to go backward before you can go forward.

Why is it necessary to remember? Because that's how we as human beings make sense of our lives. We recall and tell stories. We create narratives that have beginnings, middles, and ends. And when we connect up all the random bits in the telling, we not only see an understandable path emerging from what may at first seem like a string of randomness, we also discover and affirm what has been truly important and meaningful to us along the way.

So if you're expecting the death of a loved one, I hope you will make time to gather up photos and memorabilia. If it's possible, I hope you will share memories with the person who is sick or dying as well as others who have been part of your lives. Don't shy away from exploring bad memories as well as happier ones. Both are part of your story.

If you're expecting a significant change other than a death, exploring memories means finding ways to review the choices and moments that led you to this point. Why has the love or attachment been such a big part of your life? What has the experience been like? Which memories stand out? What will you miss most? What will you miss least? Tell the stories to others and write some of them down if you want.

Some of you might be thinking that it's too painful to explore memories. Even when you remember times that made you exquisitely happy, you're right—it can hurt if you're simultaneously aware that those times are done and gone. And remembering the bad days hurts too, for obvious reasons. But once again, the magic trick: resurrecting memories tames them (with the notable exception of traumatic memories, which are most effectively and safely explored with the help of a trained trauma counselor). When you remember and you share those memories outside of yourself, you're better able to view them in the context of your entire life, including your present and your future. They are indeed important parts of the patchwork quilt that is your life story—but they're not the whole quilt.

I promise you this: The more time and attention you devote to exploring memories and sharing and discussing them with others, the more your sense of peace will grow.

NEED 4: DEVELOP A NEW SELF-IDENTITY

We tend to think of ourselves in relation to the major relationships and attachments in our lives. You're so-and-so's child, so-and-so's spouse or partner, so-and-so's parent, so-and-so's colleague...and so on. You're a resident of _____, you are or were a _____ (career), you're a fan of _____, and you belong to groups such as _____.

But now, at least one of those major relationships or attachments that has partly defined you is coming to an end. Who will you be after the loss? Pondering and searching for answers to that question is the work of this mourning need.

This is not a simple or fast mourning need. It takes time to pick up the pieces of your former, crumbling identity and construct a new one. As with all facets of grief and mourning, there are no rewards for speed. Go at your own pace and take as much time as you need.

How you might choose to actively work on this mourning need depends on the nature of the loss. If a longtime partner is dying, for example, your identity as half of a couple as well as your daily routine must be reconsidered and created anew. If you are leaving a longtime career, you are tasked with figuring out who you "are" and what you will "do" now.

This mourning need is largely forward-looking. When you work on need 3, you look to the past. When you work on need 4, you look to the future. Change is often both a loss and an opportunity, even if it's an opportunity you would never willingly have chosen. You've come to a fork in the road with myriad branches. Which will you pick?

And that's another thing about this mourning need: You get to decide. If you muster the courage and determination to be intentional about who you will be moving forward, you can use this fork in the road to spur yourself in the direction of deeper meaning and joy.

Try asking yourself these questions:

- What have I always wanted to do or be but never got around to?

- What's on my bucket list?

- When I imagine myself at the end of my life, what will I most regret not having done?

- How can I build more mindful presence into my life?

I truly believe that each person's unique life is a once-in-infinity miracle. That includes yours, of course. I hope you will actively work on this mourning need with that understanding.

NEED 5: SEARCH FOR MEANING

This mourning need is about exploring and finding a sense of meaning and purpose, both in the attachment that is ending and in your continued living. It overlaps with the other needs because it involves reviewing your past as well as considering what you want out of life moving forward.

Already you may have found yourself trying to make sense of it all. What has given your life the most meaning? In what ways was the love or attachment that is coming to a close part of that meaning? How will you build meaning into your life from this day on?

The search for meaning takes us into spiritual territory. When we wonder why we're here, what life is all about, and what happens after we die—all common concerns during a time of loss—we're searching for meaning. It's a natural human tendency to ponder life's meaning and try to arrive at answers that give us a sense of purpose and peace.

As you work on this mourning need, you'll probably turn to religious or spiritual beliefs. You may also call those beliefs into question. It's normal to have doubts, be angry, or change your mind. This is a time of major transition and change in your life, and it's normal to discover new insights and truths.

I always encourage grieving people to prioritize their spiritual needs and make time to get in touch with their spirituality each and every day. What this looks like for you will depend on your habits and beliefs, but the bottom line is that it means doing something that nurtures your divine spark—that still, small voice inside you that whispers to you about what gives you a sense of meaning and purpose.

Your daily spiritual habits might include prayer, meditation, reading a spiritual text, yoga, communing with your garden or nature, contemplative walking, or getting lost in an activity that makes you feel deeply alive. Whatever nurtures your spirit in these ways, I recommend you spend at least ten minutes a day doing it—and preferably more.

Many people in our hectic, information-overloaded, plugged-in culture never take the time to slow down, turn inward, and listen to their spirits instead of all the noise coming at them. But especially during this period of change in your life, your spirit needs attention. Working on this mourning need will not only ease your grief, it will also help you find a reason to keep getting out of bed in the morning. And in the long run, it is what will allow you to live the rest of your precious days with as much meaning, purpose, love, and joy as possible.

NEED 6: REACH OUT FOR AND ACCEPT SUPPORT FROM OTHERS

Grief is an inner experience, but mourning is outward, and that means involving other people.

During your time of transition, you need and deserve support. Understandably, you are struggling. You may think that you can go it alone. You might believe that if you just tough it out and make it to the other side of this loss, you'll be OK. But the truth is that without the empathetic compassion of other people, you won't be OK. Not really.

Yes, you may survive, but you will likely feel lost and alone

One definition of mourning is that is the shared social response to loss. When we gather at a funeral, for example, we are mourning together. That's why funerals are so important—they help us meet all of the mourning needs we've been talking about *in the company of others*. We can acknowledge the reality of the loss, embrace the pain, explore memories, struggle with our self-identity, and search for meaning all we want, but if we never share those mourning activities with others along the way, we will never fully reconcile our grief.

I know that it can be hard to reach out for support during a period of anticipatory grief. After all, you may be in the middle of something that is hard to define and even harder to talk about. You might be unsure if what you're feeling is "normal." You might feel undeserving of attention because the ultimate loss hasn't really happened yet. But I'm here to tell you that your current grief is completely real, valid, and necessary. And there are others who will understand. Many people will empathize with and support you if you are open and honest with them.

What's more, you may be a victim of the misconception that you shouldn't have to reach out to others—they should be reaching out to *you*. The truth is that some people simply don't understand what you're going through. They either don't know the facts, or they're too busy with their own life challenges to have given your circumstances much thought. Others may know what you're going through but have no idea what they can do about it. They may be silently and distantly empathizing with you but feel at a loss about how to support you. So please, set this misconception aside and be the one to actively reach out. Once you open the door, you'll probably find at least a few people who are happy to walk through it to help you.

Now, it's true that not everyone has the capacity to be a good helper. I often talk about the rule of thirds: One-third of your friends and family will be good, nonjudgmental listeners who are supportive of your need to mourn. Another third will be neutral, neither helping nor hindering you. And the final third will make you feel worse and may judge you for your need to grieve and mourn. Turn to the first third when you are feeling your grief and need to express it.

Besides friends and family, support groups are another wonderful forum for expressing anticipatory grief. You'll find support groups online and/or in your community, especially for common loss experiences like caring for a loved one with dementia, coping with the life-threatening illness of a loved one, and living through the process of separation and divorce. Participating in a support group that is specific to your situation is often one of the most helpful, healing self-care steps you can take.

Likewise, you can also informally pair up with others who have experienced a similar loss. If you know someone who went through or is going through the same type of loss you are, give them a call. Buy them a cup of coffee or lunch and ask about their experience of loss and grief. Simply talking about shared experiences and insights can be a huge relief. It helps to know that you're not alone.

In addition to finding good listeners and empathizers, you will also benefit from regular companionship and social contact. In other words, you don't always have to be talking about your grief to feel that balm of support that is so critical. Simply maintaining friendships, neighbor relationships, volunteer acquaintances, and other ties in your network of friends and family will give you the little doses of connection and care you need to remember that you are part of a community. While I understand that your current transition circumstances may leave you with precious little time, opportunity, and energy for socializing, you can probably set aside a few minutes here and there to talk on the phone, have a text conversation, go for a walk with a friend, or invite someone over to watch a movie. Even one friendly relationship can be enough.

As you actively work on these six mourning needs—and I hope you will!—please keep in mind that you will still be working on them after the loss. It's not possible to take care of all of your grief and mourning needs preemptively. I am definitely *not* claiming that if you mourn your anticipatory grief well you will be "done" mourning and instantly at peace when the loss occurs. No. You will continue to grieve, and you will continue to need to mourn.

LOVING, LIVING, AND MOURNING AT THE SAME TIME

"I spent a lot of years trying to outrun or outsmart vulnerability by making things certain and definite, black and white, good and bad. My inability to lean into the discomfort of vulnerability limited the fullness of those important experiences that are wrought with uncertainty: love, belonging, trust, joy, and creativity, to name a few."

— Dr. Brené Brown

As we've emphasized, you are living through a difficult time of significant change. The process of the change itself is painful, and the eventual loss you are projecting is also painful. Other losses in your life were probably different. Something difficult happened and then, *wham*. You found yourself grieving and picking up the pieces after the loss. There was the Before, then there was the After.

But right now you are inhabiting the During. You're in the confusing, uncomfortable purgatory of in-between. *Limina* is the Latin word for "threshold," the transitional space betwixt and between. People generally don't like being in liminal space because of the uncertainty. It feels unstable and unsettled. Have you found yourself at times wishing that whatever is going to happen would just happen? That it could just be "over and done with" and things could "get back to normal"? This natural and understandable feeling comes from our uneasiness with During. When my own father was dying, my mother said to me, "If he doesn't die soon, I'm going to beat him to it." She deeply loved the man she'd been married to for fifty years, of course, but it was so painful to see him dwindling and to experience the extended During that she sometimes joked about hurrying things along.

But whether you like it or not, here you are, stuck in the During. How are you supposed to keep living and loving while also coping with the changing circumstances and your grief at the same time?

It's a lot to ask. And no matter what, you won't always feel like you're managing it all successfully. But the ideas in this section will help you integrate your grief into your daily life as you live and love as well as you can during the difficult During.

PRACTICE MINDFULNESS

There is a difference between existing and living. Too many people sleepwalk through life. Mindfulness is about enjoying life and making the most of it. It's about relishing our precious time on earth. But it's also about using our discerning awareness each day to spend our time fully in the now and make constructive choices.

As a death and grief educator for more than forty years, I've been around a lot of loss. Over and over again, death has taught me that life is a fantastic opportunity. It's a smorgasbord of delights, and it presents all of us with the possibilities to build loving relationships and meaningful accomplishments. It's replete with joy and yes, heartbreak. Yet whether we truly experience all of that—the delights, the relationships, the accomplishments, the joy, the heartbreak—depends on our willingness and dedication to intentional, mindful living, one day at a time.

SET YOUR INTENTIONS DAILY

No, you can't control life, but you can control a few things. One is your intentions. You get to decide how you intend to live each day. You get to imagine how your day will proceed, how you will spend your time, and, importantly, how you will respond when things happen that were not part of your plan.

Each morning I set my intentions for what I will focus on that day. Many of my intentions are not "doing"-related but instead "being"-related. For example, I may intend to be on the alert for something to be grateful for in each moment. I may intend to step away from electronics and pay attention to everything I can sense with my five senses. Or I may intend to be present to my wife and family, not worrying one way or the other about what we are "doing" or judging anything but instead simply training my awareness on our aliveness.

In grief, you may set your intention to devote some time each day to active mourning and reserving the rest of any free time in your day for living in the now, no matter what the now may bring.

EMBRACE ALLOWING

Many spiritual thinkers who are wiser than I am teach that allowing is the key to living well. We talked earlier about the illusion of control. The truth is that there are many things we can't control in our lives, even though we may foolishly try. So the better way, say the gurus, is to relinquish our illusions of control and instead accept whatever happens as it's happening.

Each day, you embrace allowing by cultivating equanimity, which is the state of being calm and composed, especially under stress. Whatever happens, happens, and it's OK. Everything belongs.

Allowing isn't the same as not caring or giving up, however. You can and should still set your intentions for the day, but at the same time, you remain flexible as the day unfolds. You remain present to the whirl of life around you, and as much as possible, you observe with wonder and gratitude.

And when bad things happen that you can't change, instead of hopelessly battling them or running away from them, you make space for them. You allow them to be, and you bear witness to them. This minimizes the pain and expands your experience of the fullness of life.

CARING FOR AND LOVING SOMEONE WHO HAS DEMENTIA

Being a caregiver to someone with dementia is often a harrowing encounter with anticipatory grief. It's physically, emotionally, cognitively, socially, and spiritually challenging. It's chockful of daily losses and compromises. And because dementia is a progressive disease, it only gets harder. I personally walked this walk with my mother for the three years leading up to her death. I always say that I mourned her twice: during her dementia decline and after she died.

In addition to applying the mourning and mindfulness practices recommended in this little book, I urge you to reach out for and accept help from as many sources as possible. Dementia caregiving is a team sport, and there are people and organizations who will help you. The book *The Dementia Care-Partner's Workbook*, written by my friend and colleague Dr. Edward G. Shaw, contains excellent, practical information and advice. I hope you will read it, too.

CARING FOR AND LOVING SOMEONE WHO IS DYING

Of course you will experience deep grief as you care for a loved one who is dying.

It can be hard to know how much to encourage that person to prolong their life. You want them to live, but you don't want them to suffer. You want to support their wishes, but you may also want them to fight…or you may want them to focus on quality of life because the physical repercussions of the fight seem too great a sacrifice.

There are no right answers, but the concept of allowing might help you. If the person who is sick makes the decisions as much as possible, your role is to allow, support, and be present with loving kindness. And as the disease progresses, you are present on any given day to offer the person who is dying comfort, care, and a listening ear. You are there to bear witness to their grief as well as yours. Those are the greatest gifts life offers.

LIVING THROUGH DIVORCE

Millions of couples each year suffer the anticipatory grief that comes with separation and impending divorce. Even if the divorce is mutually agreed upon and amicable, the process of permanently separating from a spouse typically gives rise to a range of painful thoughts and feelings, including sadness, anger, guilt, shame, and more.

It's normal to grieve the many losses that are part and parcel of divorce. You may grieve the loss of things you still love about your spouse. You may grieve the loss of a person with whom you shared a history and a significant part of your life. You may grieve the loss of a two-parent home for your children or grandchildren. You may also grieve the loss of hopes and dreams. What you originally imagined for your marriage may have never come to be. Or perhaps you grieve the loss of your dreams for a shared future.

Whatever your feelings about your divorce are, they are part of your grief, and they are normal and necessary. If your relationship with your ex-to-be is healthy, I urge you to talk through all these feelings with them as they arise in the weeks and months to come. Sharing the work of mourning along the way may help you remain friendly and, if you have children, co-parents.

LOVING AN ELDERLY PERSON

It strikes me that loving an elderly person, especially one who may be growing increasingly frail or dependent, involves living in a state of anticipatory grief. Both the elderly person and you may be grieving any decline in health and vigor as well as remaining lifespan. It can feel as if the clock is ticking—and that ticking clock represents your constant awareness that a loss is coming.

There is nothing for it but presence and being attuned to the elderly person's changing abilities and needs. If their eyesight is failing, for example, they may need more help with tasks of daily living. Your eyes become theirs. If they need regular company to stave off isolation and loneliness, you are there, and you may also be arranging for others to visit.

You are grieving and mourning, and you are also loving in the active sense of that verb. Grief and love are simply two sides of the same coin. They go together. And when you bring your awareness and expression to both of them daily, you are living the fullness of life.

AS THE LOSS HAPPENS

"Always hold fast to the present.
Every situation, indeed every moment, is of infinite value,
for it is the representative of a whole eternity."
— Johann Wolfgang von Goethe

In most anticipatory grief situations, there is an endpoint to the loss itself. There is a death or a finalizing of the divorce or a bankruptcy or a definitive, final transition of some kind. In fact, many of these turning points happen on a certain day at a certain time. After all the long weeks or even years of During, a curtain falls.

On that day, you will experience that moment of finality. And you may think that because you've been anticipating the loss for so long, you'll be prepared. That you will be braced and ready.

The truth is that we're never really ready for loss. Many, many times over the years, people who had been expecting a great loss have told me that on the day of the loss, they were taken by surprise. Sometimes things didn't go as they expected they would. Events unfolded in unanticipated or blindsiding ways. And many people felt shocked at the blow. The sharpness and magnitude of their grief stunned them.

You have probably found yourself imagining the day of the loss. It's a normal and natural thing to do. But I also hope you will remember that it's one thing to imagine and another to experience. The two will probably differ in lots of ways.

The principles we've been discussing in this book, however, will help you on that day, no matter how things unfold. If you allow and remain present, grateful, and loving, you will flow with the experience instead of against it. Holding this attitude may even open you to good and miraculous moments you never could have imagined.

On the day of the loss, you will also need help. I urge you to have one or two reliable supporters at the ready—someone who can accompany you in person if at all possible or support you closely from a distance on that day. It's a good idea to identify those people ahead of time and ask them if they will do you the favor of being by your side when the time comes. With this kind of advance permission and a little planning, many people are willing and able to step up in times of crisis. As the saying goes, a friend in need is a friend indeed.

You may be dreading the day of the loss, or you may be looking toward it with a degree of hope and relief. Actually, you will probably experience a mixture of these and other emotions as over time you wonder about that coming day. This is normal. When I caution you to manage your expectations, I don't mean to make your time of anticipation any more complicated than it already is. Instead, I hope you will trust in yourself. You are strong, you are capable, and you are resilient. How do I know this? Because you are already living through anticipatory grief, possibly under extremely challenging circumstances. And with grace, presence, and love, I know that you will be even more capable of living through the time of the loss—because you are building those very skills right now.

AFTER THE LOSS

"The reality is that you will grieve forever. You will not 'get over'
the loss...; you will learn to live with it. You will heal,
and you will rebuild yourself around the loss you have suffered.
You will be whole again, but you will never be the same.
Nor should you be the same, nor would you want to."
— Dr. Elisabeth Kübler-Ross

After the time of the loss, you will find yourself in new yet
familiar territory. You will continue to grieve, and so you
will continue to need to express your grief through active
mourning.

Some anticipatory grievers imagine or hope that by the time
the loss takes place, they will have used up all their grief.
They will be done grieving, and they will be able to move
forward with their lives, which understandably felt on hold
or stalled by the expected loss situation.

Yet the reality is that grief lasts forever. It never gets "used
up." It is never done because your love or attachment is
never truly done. BUT (and this is a big but) it does soften

and change. The process of active mourning and working on your six needs of mourning on an ongoing basis—before, during, and after the loss—is what will help you reconcile your grief.

WHAT DOES RECONCILED GRIEF MEAN?

It means that it settles into being an integrated part of your present and future. In other words, it becomes part of who you are. It no longer dominates your days but instead lives in the background, much as all of your significant past life experiences do.

Again, you get to reconciliation with the magic trick that is active mourning. Without active mourning, your grief remains unreconciled, essentially locked away and festering. People who don't actively mourn end up carrying their grief inside them. And they often go on to experience relationship troubles, anxiety, depression, and/or substance abuse issues—without realizing that it is their unreconciled grief that is causing these difficulties.

How will you know you're moving toward reconciling your grief? You'll know because you will start to feel lighter and less burdened by the loss. Other signs of reconciliation include:

• a recognition of the reality and finality of the loss

- a return to stable eating and sleeping patterns.

- a renewed sense of release from the person or thing that has left your life. You will still have thoughts and feelings about it, but you will not be preoccupied by them.

- the capacity to enjoy experiences in life that are normally enjoyable.

- the establishment of new and healthy relationships, interests, and attachments

- the capacity to live a full life without feelings of guilt or lack of self-respect

- the drive to organize and plan your life toward the future

- the serenity to become comfortable with the way things are rather than attempting to make things as they were

- the versatility to welcome more change in your life

- the awareness that you have allowed yourself to fully grieve and mourn, and you have survived.

- the awareness that you do not "get over" your grief; instead, you have a new reality, meaning, and purpose in your life

- the acquaintance of new parts of yourself that you have discovered in your grief journey

- the adjustment to new role or life changes that have resulted from the loss

- the acknowledgment that the pain of loss in an inherent part of life resulting from the ability to give and receive love

The reconciliation of grief emerges much in the way grass grows. Usually we don't check our lawns daily to see if the grass is growing, but it does grow, and soon we come to realize it's time to mow the grass again. Likewise, we don't look at ourselves each day as mourners to see how we are healing. Yet we do come to realize, over the course of months and years, that we have come a long way. We have taken some important steps toward reconciliation.

Usually there is not one great moment of "arrival" but instead subtle changes and small advancements. It's helpful to have gratitude for even very small blessings. If you are beginning to taste your food again, be thankful. If you mustered the energy to meet a friend for lunch, be grateful. If you finally got a good night's sleep, rejoice.

Even when your grief is reconciled, it will still announce itself now and then. You will be triggered by a memory, a place, a song, or a smell, and you will feel an intense wave of grief. I call these experiences griefbursts, and they are normal and natural.

Keep believing in yourself. Set your intention to reconcile your grief, and have hope that you can and will come to live and love fully again.

A FINAL WORD

"Once you choose hope, anything is possible."
— Christopher Reeve

Anticipatory grief is often a dark, painful, and confusing time of limbo. I know it's hard. I understand that you are being challenged daily by what is unfolding around you and to you as well as your inner thoughts and feelings. It is well possible that much is being asked of you right now.

But still there is hope. And besides actively mourning and practicing mindfulness, that is the one additional thing I implore you to work on.

Hope is an expectation of a good that is yet to be. It is a forward-looking feeling that sees the future as containing peace, happiness, and joy. But the secret is that hope is more than a feeling. It is an action and a practice, and I want you to think of it that way.

Just like love and mourning are best understood as actions, so is hope. You can passively wait for hope to drift by, or you cultivate it. You can grow it like a flower.

Here's how: Build pursuits, passions, and people into your daily life that make you feel hopeful. In fact, stop right now and spend a minute asking yourself, "What makes me feel hopeful? What or who gives me that buoyant sense that things can be good again, that there are things to look forward to in life?"

Whatever the answers to those questions are for you, at least one of them belongs on your schedule each and every day. Maybe it's cuddling a grandchild or meeting buddies for a game of golf. Maybe it's planning your next vacation, sharing a homecooked meal with a loved one, phoning your best friend, or praying or meditating.

In fact, I invite you to put down this book right now and plant a seed of hope. Spend five minutes doing one thing that reminds you that life offers happiness and connection.

I will be thinking about you in the months to come. I hope you will mourn actively and live and love deeply. Godspeed.

THE
ANTICIPATORY GRIEVER'S
BILL OF RIGHTS

Though you should reach out to others as you journey
through grief, you shouldn't feel obligated to accept the
unhelpful responses you may receive from some people. You
are the one who is grieving, and as such, you have certain
"rights" no one should try to take away from you.

The following list is intended both to empower you to heal
and to decide how others can and cannot help. This is not
to discourage you from reaching out to others for help, but
rather to assist you in distinguishing useful responses from
hurtful ones.

1. YOU HAVE THE RIGHT TO EXPERIENCE YOUR OWN UNIQUE GRIEF.
No one else will grieve in exactly the same way you do. So,
when you turn to others for help, don't allow them to tell
what you should or should not be feeling.

2. YOU HAVE THE RIGHT TO TALK ABOUT YOUR GRIEF.
Talking about your grief will help you cope with and

integrate it. Seek out others who will allow you to talk as much as you want, as often as you want, about your grief and loss experience. If at times you don't feel like talking, you also have the right to be silent.

3. YOU HAVE THE RIGHT TO FEEL A MULTITUDE OF EMOTIONS.

Confusion, numbness, disorientation, fear, guilt, and relief are just a few of the emotions you might feel as part of your grief journey. Others may try to tell you that feeling angry, for example, is wrong. Don't take these judgmental responses to heart. Instead, find listeners who will accept your feelings without condition.

4. YOU HAVE THE RIGHT TO BE TOLERANT OF YOUR PHYSICAL AND EMOTIONAL LIMITS.

The circumstances of this period of change will probably leave you feeling fatigued. As much as possible, respect what your body and mind are telling you. Get daily rest. Eat balanced meals. And don't allow others to push you into doing things you don't feel ready to do.

5. YOU HAVE THE RIGHT TO EXPERIENCE UNCERTAINTY.

Anticipatory grief happens during times of change and uncertainty. If you feel unsure about what's happening or what's going to happen, that's normal. It's OK to feel uncertain.

6. YOU HAVE THE RIGHT TO EMBRACE YOUR SPIRITUALITY.

Express your spirituality in ways that seem appropriate to you. Allow yourself to be around people who understand and support your religious or spiritual beliefs. If you feel angry at God, find someone to talk with who won't be critical of your feelings of hurt and abandonment.

7. YOU HAVE THE RIGHT TO SEARCH FOR MEANING.

You may find yourself wondering why things are happening as they are. Some of your questions may have answers, but some may not. And watch out for the clichéd responses some people may give you. Comments like, "It's God's will" or "Think of what you have to be thankful for" are not helpful, and you do not have to accept them.

8. YOU HAVE THE RIGHT TO TREASURE YOUR MEMORIES.

Good memories are lifelong treasures. You will always remember. Instead of ignoring your memories, find others with whom you can share them.

9. YOU HAVE THE RIGHT TO HOPE.

Your time of change and anticipatory loss will one day come to an end. In the meantime, you have the right to nurture hope about good things to come in your future.

10. YOU HAVE THE RIGHT TO MOVE TOWARD YOUR GRIEF AND HEAL.
Reconciling your grief will not happen quickly. Remember, grief is a process, not an event. Be patient and tolerant with yourself and avoid people who are impatient and intolerant with you. Neither you nor those around you must forget that significant loss changes your life forever.

The Journey Through Grief
REFLECTIONS ON HEALING | SECOND EDITION

This revised, second edition of *The Journey Through Grief* takes Dr. Wolfelt's popular book of reflections and adds space for guided journaling, asking readers thoughtful questions about their unique mourning needs and providing room to write responses.

ISBN 978-1-879651-11-1 • 152 pages • hardcover • $21.95

First Aid for Broken Hearts

Life is both wonderful and devastating. It graces us with joy, and it breaks our hearts. If your heart is broken, this book is for you. Whether you're struggling with a death, break-up, illness, unwanted life change, or loss of any kind, this book will help you both understand your predicament and figure out what to do about it.

ISBN: 978-1-61722-281-8 • softcover • $9.95

The Wilderness of Grief
A BEAUTIFUL, HARDCOVER GIFT BOOK VERSION OF
UNDERSTANDING YOUR GRIEF

The Wilderness of Grief is an excerpted version of *Understanding Your Grief*, making it approachable and appropriate for all mourners. This concise book makes an excellent gift for anyone in mourning. On the book's inside front cover is room for writing an inscription to your grieving friend.

ISBN 978-1-879651-52-4 • 112 pages • hardcover • $15.95

All Dr. Wolfelt's publications can be ordered by mail from:
Companion Press, 3735 Broken Bow Road, Fort Collins, CO 80526
(970) 226-6050 • www.centerforloss.com

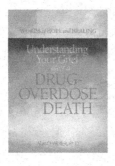

The Grief of Infertility

When you want to have a baby but are struggling with fertility challenges, it's normal to experience a range and mixture of ever-changing feelings. These feelings are a natural and necessary form of grief. Whether you continue to hope to give birth or you've stopped pursuing pregnancy, this compassionate guide will help you affirm and express your feelings about infertility.

By giving authentic attention to your grief, you will be helping yourself cope with your emotions as well as learn how to actively mourn and live fully and joyfully at the same time. This compassionate guide will show you how. Tips for both women and men are included.

ISBN: 978-1-61722-291-7 • softcover • $9.95

If You're Lonely: Finding Your Way

Ironically, if you are lonely, you're not alone. People the world over are experiencing an epidemic of loneliness. In the US, one in five of us reports feeling lonely, and almost half of seniors are lonely on a regular basis. Loneliness hurts, and it can lead to depression, addiction, physical problems, and other harmful consequences.

This compassionate guide will help you better understand your loneliness as well as the important distinction between isolation and solitude. It also offers a variety of practical suggestions for reclaiming community and building meaningful connections in ways that suit you.

978-1-61722-297-9 • softcover • $9.95

All Dr. Wolfelt's publications can be ordered by mail from:
Companion Press, 3735 Broken Bow Road, Fort Collins, CO 80526
(970) 226-6050 • www.centerforloss.com

Nature Heals: Reconciling Your Grief Through Engaging with the Natural World

When we're grieving, we need relief from our pain. Today we often turn to technology for distraction when what we really need is the opposite: generous doses of nature. Studies show that time spent outdoors lowers blood pressure, eases depression and anxiety, bolsters the immune system, lessens stress, and even makes us more compassionate. This guide to the tonic of nature explores why engaging with the natural world is so effective at helping reconcile grief. It also offers suggestions for bringing short bursts of nature time (indoors and outdoors) into your everyday life as well as tips for actively mourning in nature. This book is your shortcut to hope and healing…the natural way.

978-1-61722-301-3 • softcover • $9.95

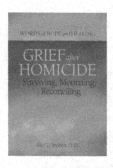

Grief After Homicide: Surviving, Mourning, Reconciling

Homicide creates a grief like no other. If someone you love died by homicide, your grief is naturally traumatic and complicated. Not only might your grief journey be intertwined with painful criminal justice proceedings, you may also struggle with understandably intense rage, regret, and despair. It's natural for homicide survivors to focus on the particular circumstances of the death as well. Whether your loved one's death was caused by murder or manslaughter, this compassionate guide will help you understand and cope with your difficult grief. It offers suggestions for reconciling yourself to the death on your own terms and finding healing ways for you and your family to mourn. After a homicide death, there is help for those left behind, and there is hope. This book will help see you through.

978-1-61722-303-7 • Softcover • $9.95

All Dr. Wolfelt's publications can be ordered by mail from:
Companion Press, 3735 Broken Bow Road, Fort Collins, CO 80526
(970) 226-6050 • www.centerforloss.com

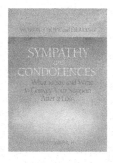

Sympathy and Condolences:
What to Say and Write to Convey Your
Support After a Loss

When someone you care about has suffered the death of a loved one or another significant loss, you want to let them know you care. But it can be hard to know what to say to them or to write in a sympathy note. This handy book offers tips for how to talk or write to a grieving person to convey your genuine concern and support. What to say, what not to say, sympathy card etiquette, how to keep in touch, and more are covered in this concise guide written by one of the world's most beloved grief counselors. You'll turn to it again and again, not only after a death but during times of divorce or break-ups, serious illness, loss of a pet, job change or loss, traumatic life events, major life transitions that are both happy and sad, and more.

978-1-61722-305-1 • $9.95 • softcover

All Dr. Wolfelt's publications can be ordered by mail from:
Companion Press, 3735 Broken Bow Road, Fort Collins, CO 80526
(970) 226-6050 • www.centerforloss.com